P9-CLC-010

African-American Heroes

Will Smith

Stephen Feinstein

Enslow Elementary
an imprint of
Enslow Publishers, Inc.
40 Industrial Road
Box 398
Berkeley Heights, NJ 07922
USA

 http://www.enslow.com

Words to Know

comedian (cuh-MEE-dee-un)—Someone whose job it is to tell jokes and make people laugh.

DJ—A person who plays recorded music at a party or club. "DJ" is short for "disc jockey."

Grammy Award—A prize for the best recorded music.

nominate (NAH-mih-nayt)—To recommend someone for an honor or award.

producing (pro-DOO-sing)—Making or creating something.

rap—Rhyming words performed with music.

rapper—Someone who performs rap.

science fiction—Stories based on imaginary scientific events.

Enslow Elementary, an imprint of Enslow Publishers, Inc.

Enslow Elementary® is a registered trademark of Enslow Publishers, Inc.

Library of Congress Cataloging-in-Publication Data

Feinstein, Stephen.
    Will Smith / Stephen Feinstein.
        p. cm. — (African-American heroes)
    Includes index.
    ISBN-13: 978-0-7660-2765-7
    ISBN-10: 0-7660-2765-1
    1. Smith, Will, 1968—-Juvenile literature. 2. Actors—United States—Biography—Juvenile literature. 3. Rap musicians—United States—Biography—Juvenile literature. 4. African American actors—Biography—Juvenile literature. I. Title.
    PN2287.S612F45 2007
    791.4302'8092—dc22
    [B]
                        2006034067

Printed in the United States of America

10 9 8 7 6 5 4 3 2

Illustration Credits: AP/Wide World, pp. 4, 5, 13, 18, back cover; Classmates.com, pp. 3, 8; Digital Vision, p. 6; © DreamWorks/courtesy Everett Collection, p. 7; Everett Collection, pp. 3, 11, 15, 17 (upper and lower right), 20; Michael Germana/Everett Collection, p. 21; iStockphoto.com, p. 10; Erik C. Pendzich/Rex Features, courtesy Everett Collection, p. 1; S. Sarac/Everett Collection, p. 19; Shutterstock, pp. 6–7; Time Life Pictures/Getty Images, pp. 3, 12; 20th Century Fox Film Corp./courtesy Everett Collection, pp. 3, 17 (upper and lower left); © Warner Bros./courtesy Everett Collection, p. 2.

Cover Illustration: Michael Germana/Everett Collection.

Contents

Chapter 1 The Class Clown

Will Smith was born on September 25, 1968, in Philadelphia, Pennsylvania. When he was little, his mother, Caroline, and his father, Willard, used to read to him.

Will's favorite books were by Dr. Seuss. They were filled with rhymes and were a lot of fun.

Like lots of kids, Will loved Dr. Seuss books.

Will Smith grew up to be a famous rapper and actor.

Will's grandmother Helen Bright took him to church on Sundays. One day she got Will to play a part in a church holiday play. He liked acting on the stage.

Will also learned how to play the piano. His parents loved music. They wanted Will and his brother and two sisters to play musical instruments and to sing. Will dreamed about becoming a performer.

Will and his family liked playing music, like these students.

This is Philadelphia, the city Will lived in.

Eddie Murphy, Will's favorite comedian, did the voice of Donkey in the movie *Shrek*.

Will's favorite star was the **comedian** Eddie Murphy. Will loved to watch him on the TV show *Saturday Night Live*. Will's family was also very funny. At dinnertime, everyone joked and laughed a lot. Once Will learned that he could make people laugh, he never stopped trying.

"How does this thing work, anyway?" This sentence was under Will's high school yearbook photo.

This is Will's class photo from his high school yearbook. He liked to joke around, but he also did well in school.

At school, Will enjoyed being the class clown. His funny stories and funny faces made the other kids laugh. His friends called him "Prince" because he was so funny and so smart.

Will loved being the center of attention. But he knew when to stop fooling around. His parents expected Will to do well in school, and he did.

Chapter 2

Will Becomes a Rapper

When Will was twelve, he became interested in **rap** music. Rap seemed to be a perfect way to show his feelings about life. Will enjoyed being a **DJ** at parties, playing records for the other kids. But what he really wanted to do was perform rap music. Will had loved rhyming words ever since he was little. Soon he was putting his own words to rhythm.

DJs make interesting sounds with records on turntables.

When Will was sixteen, he met another DJ named Jeff Townes at a party. The two became close friends. They began performing rap music at parties and clubs in Philadelphia. Jeff wrote the music and Will wrote the words. They called themselves DJ Jazzy Jeff and the Fresh Prince.

Jeff Townes and Will became good friends.

Jeff and Will perform at a concert.

Once Will and Jeff began making records, they became famous. Their first album was called *Rock the House*. It sold 600,000 copies in 1987. The next year, their album *He's the DJ, I'm the Rapper* sold over a million copies.

In January 1989, Will and Jeff won prizes for the Best Rap Album and Best Rap Artist. In February, the two became the first **rappers** to win a **Grammy Award**. Their hit song "Parents Just Don't Understand" was named Best Rap Single.

DJ Jazzy Jeff and the Fresh Prince won two prizes at the American Music Awards in 1989.

Chapter 3

The Fresh Prince of Bel-Air

Will's success as a rapper had made him a millionaire. But now he wanted to try something new. He wanted to be an actor.

In 1989, Will met a man named Benny Medina. Benny had an idea for a TV show. It would be about a young African American who moves from Philadelphia to live with rich relatives in Bel-Air, California. Benny wanted Will to star in the show.

The show *The Fresh Prince of Bel-Air* was a big hit. Will was a good actor, and he was also very funny. On the show, Will played a fun-loving, street-smart young African American. The series ran from 1990 to 1996.

Will enjoyed playing a funny part in *The Fresh Prince of Bel-Air*.

Will with the actors who played his family on the TV show.

15

Chapter 4

Will Becomes a Movie Star

While Will was still working on the TV show, he began acting in movies. His first movie role was in *Where the Day Takes You* in 1992.

Will then appeared in the movies *Six Degrees of Separation* and *Bad Boys*. In the movie *Independence Day* in 1996, Will played a brave fighter pilot who helped defeat invaders from outer space. Will had been a big fan of the *Star Trek* TV series. He was happy to act in a **science-fiction** film. He later appeared in two more science-fiction films: *Men in Black* in 1997 and *I, Robot* in 2004.

INDEPENDENCE DAY

MB
MEN IN BLACK

i,ROBOT

Shark Tale

Will and his son Trey at a basketball game.

In 1992, Will married Sheree Zampino. In December, their son, Willard Christopher Smith III, was born. They called him Trey (pronounced "tray"), which is a nickname for "third."

Will's marriage to Sheree ended in 1995. But he stayed close to his son. Trey was in the video for one of Will's most famous songs, "Just the Two of Us."

In 1997, Will married the actress Jada Pinkett. They later had two children, a boy named Jaden and a girl named Willow.

Will and his wife Jada with their son Jaden and daughter Willow.

Will played the famous boxer
Muhammad Ali.

In 2000, Will played the great boxer Muhammad Ali in the movie *Ali*. He was **nominated** for an Academy Award. Will did not win, but he was proud of the hard work he did and how good the movie was.

Will continues to act and to rap. And in 2003, he and Jada started **producing** a new TV show, *All of Us*. It is about a family very much like theirs.

Will Smith tells young people to believe in themselves, get a good education, and follow their dreams.

Will's Own Words

"I don't know what my calling is, but I want to be here for a bigger reason. I strive to be like the greatest people who have ever lived."

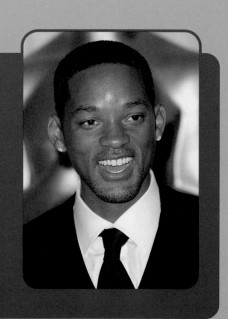

Timeline

1968—Will is born in Philadelphia on September 25.

1984—Will and Jeff Townes begin performing rap.

1989—Will and Jeff win a Grammy Award for their song "Parents Just Don't Understand."

1990–1996—Will stars in the TV show *The Fresh Prince of Bel-Air*.

1992—Will appears in the movie *Where the Day Takes You*.

2001—Will is nominated for an Academy Award for Best Actor for playing the boxer Muhammad Ali in the movie *Ali*.

2004—Will stars in the movie *I, Robot* and does one of the voices for *Shark Tale*.

2005—Will stars in the movie *Hitch* and makes the solo rap album *Lost and Found*.

Learn More

Books

Corrigan, Jim. *Will Smith*. Philadelphia: Mason Crest Publishers, 2006.

Greene, Meg. *Will Smith*. Philadelphia: Chelsea House, 2001.

Hatch, Thomas. *A History of Hip-Hop: The Roots of Rap*. Bloomington, Minn.: Red Brick Learning, 2006.

Web sites

Will Smith's official Web site
<http://www.willsmith.com>

Web site about Will Smith and Jeff Townes
<http://www.jazzyjefffreshprince.com>

Index